The Leaving Morning

story by **ANGELA JOHNSON**   *paintings by* **DAVID SOMAN**

 HOUGHTON MIFFLIN   BOSTON • MORRIS PLAINS, NJ

California • Colorado • Georgia • Illinois • New Jersey • Texas

To SANDY PERLMAN
and good times
—A.J.

To EUGENIE,
a restless family member
—D.S.

THE LEAVING happened on a soupy, misty morning,
when you could hear the street sweeper.
Sssshhhshsh....

We pressed our faces against the hall window and left cold lips on the pane.

3

It was the leaving morning.
Boxes of clothes,
toys,
dishes,
and pictures of us everywhere.

The leaving had been long because we'd packed
days before and said good-bye
to everybody we knew....

Our friends....

8

The grocer....

Everybody in our building....

And the cousins, especially the cousins.

We said good-bye to the cousins all day long.

Mama said the people in a truck would move us
and take care of everything we loved,
on the leaving morning.

We woke up early and had hot cocoa from the deli across the street.
I made more lips on the deli window
and watched for the movers on the leaving morning.

We sat on the steps and
watched the movers.
They had blue moving clothes on
and made bumping noises on the stairs.
There were lots of whistles
and "Watch out, kids."

Got me a moving hat and a kiss on the head
from Miss Mattie, upstairs.
And on the leaving morning she told me
to watch myself in the new place when I crossed
the street, and think of her.

I sat between my mama and daddy,
holding their hands.
My daddy said in a little while we'd be someplace
we'd love.

So I left lips on the front window of our apartment,
and said good-bye to our old place,
on the leaving morning.